C.2

COWS MOO!

Pam Scheunemann

Consulting Editor, Diane Craig, M.A./Reading Specialist

ABDO
Publishing Company

Published by ABDO Publishing Company, 8000 West 78th Street, Edina, Minnesota 55439.

Printed in the United States.

Editor: Katherine Hengel
Content Developer: Nancy Tuminelly
Cover and Interior Design and Production: Oona Gaarder-Juntti, Mighty Media
Photo Credits: Photodisc, ShutterStock

Library of Congress Cataloging-in-Publication Data

Scheunemann, Pam, 1955-
  Cows moo! / Pam Scheunemann.
    p. cm. -- (Animal sounds)
  ISBN 978-1-60453-569-3
  1. Dairy cattle--Juvenile literature. 2. Cows--Juvenile literature. I. Title.

SF208.S34 2009
636.2'142--dc22

                    2008033919

SandCastle™ Level: Transitional

SandCastle™ books are created by a team of professional educators, reading specialists, and content developers around five essential components—phonemic awareness, phonics, vocabulary, text comprehension, and fluency—to assist young readers as they develop reading skills and strategies and increase their general knowledge. All books are written, reviewed, and leveled for guided reading, early reading intervention, and Accelerated Reader® programs for use in shared, guided, and independent reading and writing activities to support a balanced approach to literacy instruction. The SandCastle™ series has four levels that correspond to early literacy development. The levels are provided to help teachers and parents select appropriate books for young readers.

Emerging Readers
(no flags)

Beginning Readers
(1 flag)

Transitional Readers
(2 flags)

Fluent Readers
(3 flags)

SandCastle™ would like to hear from you. Please send us your comments and suggestions.
sandcastle@abdopublishing.com

Cows are quite amazing.

Holstein cows are usually black and white. They are dairy cattle.

They do a lot of grazing.

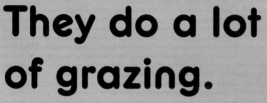

Cows spend up to eight hours a day eating.

Calves drink milk when they are born.

Adult cows can drink up to 50 gallons (190 L) of water a day.

Adults eat grass, hay, and corn.

The stomach of a cow has four compartments. Each compartment has a different purpose.

Cows will chew and chew and chew.

Cows are a kind of ruminant. Ruminant animals burp up their food and chew it again.

When cows talk,
they say moo!

Cows communicate by mooing in different ways.

Cows see motion very well.

Cows can see almost all the way around themselves without moving their heads.

They also have a great sense of smell.

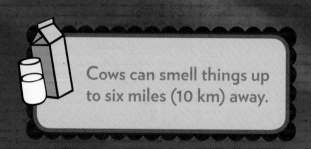

Cows can smell things up to six miles (10 km) away.

Cows use their tails to swat at flies.

In the fields, watch out for cow pies!

Cow pie is another term for cow manure. Farmers use manure to fertilize their fields.

Have you heard
a cow say moo?
I think cows are
great, don't you?

Glossary

amazing (p. 3) – causing wonder or surprise.

communicate (p. 13) – to share ideas, information, or feelings.

compartment (p. 8) – one of the separate parts of a space that has been divided.

dairy cattle (p. 3) – cows that are raised to produce milk for humans.

fertilize (p. 21) – to put a substance such as manure on land to make it richer and to make crops grow better.

graze (p. 4) – to eat grass that is growing in a field.

imitate (p. 24) – to copy or mimic someone or something.

manure (p. 21) – animal waste.

ruminant (p. 11) – an animal that digests its food in steps.

Animal Sounds Around the World

Cows sound the same no matter where they live. But the way that humans imitate them depends on what language they speak. Here are some examples of how people around the world make cow sounds:

English – moo   **French** – meuh
German – mmuuh   **Greek** – moo
Japanese – mau mau   **Spanish** – muuu